PORTLAND, MAINE

Cape Elizabeth to Freeport

A Photographic Portrait

Other titles in the *Photographic Portrait* series:

Cape Ann
Kittery to the Kennebunks
The White Mountains
The Mystic Coast, Stonington to New London
The Rhode Island Coast
Upper Cape Cod
Mid and Lower Cape Cod
The Berkshires
The Champlain Valley
Boston's South Shore
Naples, Florida

First published in the United States of America by
PilotPress Publishers, Inc.
110 Weschester Road
Newton, Massachusetts 02458
Telephone: (617) 332-0703
http://www.PilotPress.com

and

Twin Lights Publishers, Inc.
10 Hale Street
Rockport, Massachusetts 01966
Telephone: (978) 546-7398
http://www.twinlightspub.com

ISBN 1-885435-22-3

10 9 8 7 6 5 4 3 2 1

Book design by
SYP Design & Production
http://www.sypdesign.com

Front Cover Photo by: David Kirkwood
Back Cover Photos by: Claudia Dricot, Elizabeth Hutz,
William O'Donnell, and William Mattern

Printed in China

ACKNOWLEDGMENT

PilotPress and Twin Lights Publishers wish to thank all of the photographers who submitted their work for our consideration. Because of space limitations, we were unable to include many excellent photographs in *PORTLAND, MAINE: A Photographic Portrait*. The Portland area's natural beauty provided numerous interesting subjects, for both professional and amateur photographers, to record.

Special thanks go to the judges of the Portland, Maine Photograph Contest. A Maine native, Bob Moorehead is a retired newspaper reporter working for several years at *The Portland Press Herald*. He is also a photographer and editor who has published features on history, travel and sports in regional and national magazines. He lives on Paris Hill in South Paris, Maine.

Foster Shibles is a retired school superintendent who has served in several Maine communities throughout his career. He is an avid outdoorsman, naturalist and photographer. He divides his time between homes in Boothbay and in Harrison, Maine.

Lisa Patey has been involved in photography for most of her life. As well as being a wife, mother of two girls, and a career woman, she is also an accomplished award—winning photographer living in Kennebunk, Maine. Her photographs have been published in several Maine publications.

We extend our appreciation to Rockport Publishers, of 33 Commercial Street, Gloucester, MA 01930, for providing the aerial photographs.

We are grateful to Bob Moorehead who has written the captions for the photographs in *PORTLAND, MAINE: A Photographic Portrait*. He has found evocative titles and added facts to bring out the history and local color for each photograph. He has added dimension to this book.

Finally, our thanks go to Sara Day who has created yet another beautiful book.

CONTENTS

INTRODUCTION

Portland's hometown poet, Henry Wadsworth Longfellow, never allowed his boyhood surroundings to fade from his memory. The images were clear and dear. In 1855 he wrote:

"Often I think of the beautiful town
    That is seated by the sea;
 Often in thoughts go up and down
The pleasant streets of that dear old town
    And my youth comes back to me."

Portland schoolchildren memorized the lines of "My Lost Youth" for decades and seemed to relish the recitals the older they grew. Professor Longfellow was nostalgic and a romantic, spirits which to this day befit his birthplace and define it to a considerable extent.

For Portland is a city with a history, with cobblestones and bricks and stately dowager-like mansions with stories to tell. Things have happened here: wars and trade, rum and sugar, politics and fires, temperance and restoration. It is Maine's largest municipality, its largest and oldest port. Tankers and container ships come and go. The ferries are in and out, and the fishing boats never stop working. It is the state's banking and legal center. (At one point in the mid-twentieth century, there were more lawyers per population in Portland than in Washington, D.C.)

Englishmen first settled the Stroudwater section of the city in the mid-1660s. The town had grown to 2,000 residents and was still called Falmouth when, in October, 1775, a British fleet commanded by Capt. Henry Mowat started an eight-hour bombardment. The action destroyed 400 buildings and hardened an already staunch resistence to British rule.

Part of the city burned again in 1866 and was again rebuilt. The great Irish, Italian and Jewish immigration waves of the nineteenth century embraced Portland as they did other east coast cities.

During World War II, shipyards in Portland and South Portland operated around the clock building Liberty Ships. Men and women came from all over Maine and northern New England to work in the yards, crowding into every nook and cranny in the city and its suburbs. The port teemed with activity, serving as a major jumping-off spot for North Atlantic convoys and earning a reputation as a "sailor's town."

By the 1960s, a young, energetic cadre of civic leaders and municipal officers launched a restoration and revitalization of Portland. The effort extended over nearly two decades and included a massive harbor clean-up, waterfront restoration, public housing construction and infrastructure projects. The Old Port section blossomed and bloomed and the downtown was revitalized. Cultural and educational institutions became prominent features.

Longfellow's beautiful town is nearly 150 years into the future, still seated in the same place, still boasting pleasant streets and the beauty and mystery of the ships and the magic of the sea. There may even be a Spanish sailor with bearded lips.

Imagine Henry himself turning the pages of this book and engaging his senses in the artistry that camera, film and the photographer's eye can render, engaging the colors and images and suggestions of stories to be told. Imagine him marveling at his dear old town and the countryside and seashore that he never forgot.

It is now as it was then, enough to inspire poetry.

FIRST PRIZE

Second Floor, Fort Gorges

Scott Connor

NIKON N90S
KODAK ELITECHROME SELECT 100

Fort Gorges, one of seven forts
protecting Portland Harbor,
was started in 1858. It was
made obsolete before it was fin-
ished by the perfection of rifled
cannon used in the Civil War.
The Fort sets atop Hog Island
Ledge, and is maintained by the
city of Portland.

SECOND PRIZE (*opposite*)

**Yarmouth Boatyard,
Royal River**

Michael Leonard

CANON A-1

The night comes alive in dramatic
fashion in Michael Leonard's
prize-winning composition of a
storm approaching the Yarmouth
Boatyard on the Royal River.

Sunrise on Eastern Promenade

Matt Brown
CANON EOS
KODACHROME 64

Dawn begins to appear in the sky
over the Eastern Promenade.
Peaks and Great Diamond Islands
are beyond the boats at anchor.

Christmas Window

William O'Donnell

Images and texture are everywhere
in an Old Port shop window that
is sure to entice passing shoppers.

HONORABLE MENTION

The Cape Classic

Elizabeth Hutz
NIKON F2A
KODACHROME 64

Originally the site of two lighthouses built in 1824, the New England coastal classic near Dyer Point at the tip of Cape Elizabeth was rebuilt in 1874. It became a single light in 1924 but has never ceased being a favorite model of artists and photographers.

PORTLAND IS A
CITY WITH A
HISTORY, WITH
COBBLESTONES
AND BRICKS
AND STATELY
DOWAGER-LIKE
MANSIONS
WITH STORIES
TO TELL.

CAPE ELIZABETH
SOUTH PORTLAND
PORTLAND

Lobster Traps

Matt Brown

CANON EOS
FUJI VELVIA 150

Kettle Cove in Cape Elizabeth, serves as an anchorage for lobster-men. Their traps are a testimony to the hardworking, coastal tradition of drawing a livelihood from the sea.

Classic View

Elizabeth Hutz
NIKON F2A
KODACHROME 64

Rebuilt in 1874, the beauty of the
New England coastal classic at the
tip of Cape Elizabeth is inhanced
by glorious wild flowers.

Summer in Kettle Cove

Matt Brown

CANON EOS
FUJI PROVIA 100F

Photographer Matt Brown makes a study of Kettle Cove in Cape Elizabeth, from goldenrod contrasting the rocky shore to boats heading seaward to pull traps at the dawn of another day.

Spashes of Color

Matt Brown

CANON EOS
FUJI PROVIA 100F

Goldenrod and lichen cling to
the rocks adding color to the
shores at Kettle Cove in Cape
Elizabeth.

Cauldron at the Cape's Tip *(opposite)*

Penny Skolfield

OLYMPUS OMG
KODAK 200

A raging surge of wave and
wind strikes the rocks below
the lighthouse at Two Lights.
The fury of high winds and
heavy seas battering a coast
line is one of nature's awesome
sights to behold—and a sight
to be seen from a safe distance.

Red Sky in the Morning *(top)*

Stephen Raymo
CANON ELAN II E
FUJICHROME

The eastern sky serves as a warning to mariners as it silhouettes the tower and the light keepers buildings of the Cape Elizabeth light at Two Lights State Park.

Beach Roses *(bottom)*

Matt Brown
CANON EOS
FUJI PROVIA 100F

Mother Nature defies granite and salt air to enliven the coastline of Cape Elizabeth. Here, beach roses help decorate Two Lights State Park.

Serene Anchorage

Matt Brown
CANON EOS
FUJI VELVIA 50

Boats are anchored in the calm waters of Kettle Cove in Cape Elizabeth, where Maine's centuries-old fishing industry continues today.

Cold Morning at Pine Point
(above)

Timothy Byrne
NIKON F4
KONICA VELOR

A lobster boat, at anchor amid ice slabs at Pine Point, may be getting the day off as a concession to the weather. Although the summer months are busiest for lobstermen, many continue throughout the winter to pull traps when conditions are favorable. The extremes of seasons are reflected in the price.

The Cape Light by Day *(left)*

John Williams
NIKON 6006
KODAK GOLD 200

The light house near Dyer Point in Cape Elizabeth marks the southwest entry to Casco Bay and Portland Harbor. Despite the light's presence, the spiney northeastern shoreline of the Cape has claimed a number of sizable ships.

A Field at Maxwell's Farm

Claudia Dricot
NIKON N90
SENSIA II 100

Long before it became one of the state's most prestigious addresses, Cape Elizabeth was a farming community supplying the grocers of Portland and vicinity. Turn of the century summer homes along the shoreline evolved into gracious, year round residences and a post World War II building boom turned farmland into lots and streets.

**Portland Head Light
with Roses** *(opposite)*

Lila Kirkwood
MINOLTA 700
KODAK ELITE 100

Another face to Mother Nature,
the quiet beauty of coastal
roses, nestles in contrast to
spiney rocks and surf just a
stone's throw away. The
towering light seems to
provide a barrier between
the two extremes.

Blue Waters *(above)*

Matt Brown
CANON EOS
FUJI VELVIA 50

A lone lobster boat sits steady
in Kettle Cove.

Fog Over Portland Head Light *(opposite)*

Michael Leonard
CANON A 1
KODAK 160

As vessels make their way in on a foggy night, Portland Head Light is at its most comforting and appreciated.

Snow at Spring Point Light

David Kirkwood
MINOLTA 700
KODAK ELITE 100

Winter covers the rocky path to Spring Point Light with a blanket of fresh snow.

The View From Portland Observatory

Paula Abbott
KALIMAR 90-1000
FUJI 100

Probably the best view of Portland can be had from the Portland Observatory on Congress Street atop Munjoy Hill.

Inside Fort Gorges

Scott Conner

NIKON N 90S
KODAK ELITE CHROME
SELECT 100

Fort Gorges, reachable only by
private watercraft, sets atop
Hog Island Ledge. It is maintained by the city of Portland.

Cathedral of the Immaculate Conception *(above and opposite)*

Scott Conner
NIKON N 90S
FUJICHROME VELVIA 50

The spires of the Cathedral of the Immaculate Conception stand as well-recognized landmarks in the downtown area between Congress Street and Cumberland Avenue. The church complex once housed an elementary school and convent and remains one of the anchors of community life on the east end of the city.

**Back Bay at Baxter Boulevard,
4:30 A.M.** *(above)*

Mike Leonard
CANON A-1
KODACHROME 64

Dawn breaks over Back Cove
and the peninsula.

Nitelite *(left)*

Michael Leonard
CANON A-1
30 SECOND EXPOSURE

Guiding tankers, ferries and
returning fishing boats,
Portland Head Light helps
ship traffic navigate the south
passage between Cushing
Island and the Cape shore.

Portland Head Light and the Scotia Prince

Scott Conner

NIKON N 50
KODAK ELIRECHROME

The Scotia Prince passes below Portland Head Light on the return voyage from Halifax, Nova Scotia. The luxury ferry service, first launched in the late 1970s, is popular with tourists during the summer season.

After a Nor'easter *(following page)*

David Kirkwood

MINOLTA 700
KODAK ELITE 100

On a clear day, and even following in the wake of a Nor'easter's passge, it is easy to see why the scene at Portland Head is a favorite of artists, photographers and tourists.

Number 8

Kelvin Edwards

CANON F-1
FUJICOLOR 100

Aids to navigation such as this buoy are strategically placed throughout the harbor and Casco Bay by the Coast Guard.

Spring Point Marina *(below)*

Matt Brown

CANON EOS
FUJI PROVIA 100 F

Reflected in the waters of the South Portland side of the Harbor are the docks of busy Spring Point Marina.

Clear and Calm

Scott Conner

NIKON N50
KODAK ELITECHROME SELECT 100

The view from the deck of the Scotia Prince boasts the vast and beautiful Atlantic waters.

**Full Moom Rising over
Portland Head** *(opposite)*

David Kirkwood
MINOLTA 700
KODAK ELITE 100

Nature's ultimate light house
hangs over Portland Head, illu-
minating the night for sailors
returning to port.

Queen Ann's Lace

Matt Brown
CANON EOS
FUJI PROVIA 100F

As spring turns to summer on
Cape Elizabeth, delicate wild
flowers blanket Two Lights
State Park.

Portland Skyline *(above)*

Mike Leonard
CANON A-1

In the dark of night, Portland Harbor mirrors the city's Old Port and Downtown business section. Much of the city sits on a peninsula, with the harbor and Fore River on the south and west sides, Casco Bay to the northeast and Back Cove to the north.

Becky's Diner *(left)*

Matt Brown
CANON EOS REBEL 2000
FUJI VELVIA 50

A landmark catering to the working waterfront as well as the carriage trade, Becky's Diner opens early and closes late.

Beginning of the Day

Beverly Phillips

CANON TX
KODAK 400

Portland, the suburbs and Casco
Bay awakens to another blaze of
glory. But you have to get an early
start to catch such a view.

Early Morning

David Kirkwood
MINOLTA 700
KODAK ELITE 100

The rocky shore of Portland Head Light is bathed in the rays of the morning sun. This quintissentially New England scene is a favorite of artists, photographers and tourists alike.

Spring Point *(top)*

John Williams
NIKON N 70
KODAK GOLD 100

Spring Point Light in South Portland went into service in 1897 and was automated in 1934. It was connected to the mainland by a breakwater in 1951.

Boats at Boardwalk *(bottom)*

John Williams
NIKON N 70
KODAK GOLD 200

It is easy for boaters and yachtsmen to find reasons to like Portland Harbor. Wharf and marina facilities and the proximity to downtown make it a must-stopover to those on sailing vacations along the Maine coast. For many, a berth at Dimillo's is a summer-long haven.

Commercial Street

Kelvinc. Edwards
CANON F-1
FUJICOLOR 100

Commercial Street is a bustling
part of the Portland waterfront.
Here, creative signage enhances
the granite face of this centuries-
old building.

Portland Waterfront *(above)*

Kelvinc. Edwards
CANON F-1
FUJICOLOR 100

The Portland waterfront is a mixed blend of ship chandlers and outfitters, fish wholesalers, restaurants, shops, groceries, hardware stores and condominiums.

Around the Old Port *(right)*

William Mattern
CANON REBEL
AGFACHROME

Perhaps the quintessential image of Portland is one of wharves, fishing boats and brick buildings, some very new and others dating to the mid-nineteenth century or earlier.

Portland Public Market

Elizabeth Hutz

NIKON F 2A
VELVIA 50

Portland's Public Market opened in 1998 in quarters between Congress Street and Cumberland Avenue off Monument Square. The market has an extraordinary range of vendors and products. It is one of several non-profit ventures initiated in the downtown area by the late philanthropist Elizabeth Noyes.

Merrill Memorial Library

Scott Conner

NIKON N 90S
FUJICHROME VELVIA 50

The gardens at Merrill Memorial Library help to brighten a summer day.

Portland Head Light in Winter
(above)

Ross Geredien
CANON EOS A-2
FUJI VELVIA

A light dusting of snow blan-
kets the Portland Head Light.

Dramatic Skies

Stephen Raymo
CANON ELAN II E
FUJICHROME

Sunlight plays upon the rocks
at Spring Point Light, painting
a golden path to the beacon.

Starry Night

Michael Leonard
CANON A-1
FUJI 200 SUPRA

Spectators besiege the city from miles away to behold the fireworks shows on the Fourth of July. From the Eastern Prom to boat decks in the Bay to the rooves of parking garages, there's hardly a bad seat.

Sunrise *(opposite)*

Charles Boothby

Lobstermen prepare to start their day as the sun rises. At the start of the year 2000, the catch had never been better. More than 2.7 million lobsters were harvested along the Maine coast in 1999, an increase of 1.2 million since 1985.

Fort Williams

William O'Donnell

A mosaic of cut granite and
stone frames stands like a monument at Fort Williams in
Cape Elizabeth. The Fort, now
a park, was operated by the
Army in a number of capacities
into the 1960s.

**"Millenium Dawn" at
Portland Head Light**

David Bowie
NIKON N 70
KODAK GOLD 200

Silhouetted by the sunrise of
January 1, 2000, the light
might be imagined guiding in a
new millenium. The site is one
of the state's most popular subjects for artists and photographers. From the hurricane deck,
some 200 islands come into
view across Casco Bay.

"For Here or To Go?"

Melanie Alden-Roberts
MINOLTA X 370
KODAK GOLD 200

Boone's Restaurant on Custom House pier has been a landmark on the waterfront for decades. Around the corner is the Lobster Pound for those who do their own cooking.

Row it, Sail it, or . . .

William Mattern
CANON REBEL 28-800 AUTO
FUJICOLOR 100

Like a couple of harbor cabs left idling at the curb, somebody's transportation awaits them beside Custom House Wharf.

Winter Charm *(opposite)*

Douglas Leitch

CANON F 1
FUJICOLOR 100

In the wake of a snow storm,
Portland Head Light is covered
with a brilliant white coating—
a delight to the eye.

Done Workin'

Melanie Alden-Roberts

MONOLTA X 370
KODAK GOLD 200

The tide is out, the crates are
stacked and the work is done
for another day at Harbor Fish
Market. Time to take a little
break just down the street.

Full Moon

Douglas Leitch
CANON F 1
FUJICOLOR 100

Spring Point light resembles a Christmas Tree as it goes about its job on a night when it has help from a full moon and lights on the far shore.

Light Station Compass

Marcella Wagner
CANON EOS II
KODAK ROYAL GOLD

On the granite beside the Coast Guard light station, a compass is ready to serve anyone who is uncertain as to which way to go.

Amato's Restaurant, Old Port

Paula Abbott
KALIMAR K 90-1000
FUJI 100

Amato's Restaurant, located on the Old Port in early Autumn.

Portland Harbor

Diane Hudson
NIKON N 50
FUJI SENSIA 100

An ariel view of a bustling Portland Harbor. A harbor clean-up in the early 1970s led to a surge of waterfront development.

Breakwater Light *(above)*

John Williams

NIKON 6006
KODAK GOLD 100

A lobster boat passes by Spring Point Light in South Portland.

Chandler's Wharf *(right)*

Matt Brown

CANON EOS
KODACHROME 64

The condominiums at Chandler's Wharf off Commercial Street were among a number of waterfront projects developed in the early 1980s. A city-imposed moritorium on residential construction was aimed at retaining a working waterfront.

A View from Deering Oaks *(opposite)*

Charles Boothby

Deering Park is the largest in Portland and has a stand of historic old white oaks. The nearby Parkside neighborhood is overshadowed by Maine Medical Center.

Canoeists on Deering Pond *(above)*

Scott Conner

NIKON N 50
AGFA ULTRA 50

Canoeists in Deering Oaks Pond prepare for the City's Employee Appreciation Day and stay out of the reach of the fountain. The pond is a favorite of ice skaters in the winter.

Deering Oaks Park Bridge *(bottom)*

Janet Pullyard

Cool and green, this footbridge provides a shady spot on a summer afternoon.

Deering Oaks Park *(top)*

Scott D. Conner

NIKON N50
AGFA ULTRA 50

Brilliant red flowers soak up the afternoon sun at Deering Oaks Park.

President Clinton at the Sea Dogs *(bottom)*

Beverly Phillips

CANON TX
KODAK 400

It wasn't opening day (the weather was much better), but having the President to toss a few pitches seemed like a good idea. The Eastern League Portland Sea Dogs play at Hadlock Field near Deering Oaks.

Pleasant Street

Michael Leonard
CANON A-1
FUJI 200 SUPRA

A decorative gate along Pleasant Street gets dressed up for the summer by Mother Nature.

Middle at Exchange

Jenifer Bourque

At the corner of Middle and Exchange, the Canal Bank building (the bank has long since been absorbed by others) is as much apart of the neighborhood as always. Pedestrian walkways were enhanced between Middle up to Federal and Monument Square.

Boardwalk *(opposite)*

John Williams
NIKON N 70
KODAK GOLD 200

Wharf and marina facilities and the proximity to downtown make Portland Harbor a must-stopover to those on sailing vacations along the Maine coast.

Downtown *(above)*

Jennifer Bourque

Portland rarely diverts from its architectual heritage. Here, on Market Street, except for the cars, it might be the turn of the century.

Masonry and Art Live On *(left)*

Mark Conley
RICOH
FUJI 400 SUPRA

In the older sections of the city, evidence of artisans' dedication to detail is in abundance, and a treasury the city is determined to preserve.

Preserving the Past

Jennifer Bourque

The core of Portland's downtown, just outside the Old Port section, has undergone substantial rebuilding, change and enhancement in the past three decades. But "the more things change, the more they have stayed the same," in most instances.

The Limousine *(top)*

Jennifer Bourque

An enterprising horseman finds his fares along Commercial Street at the entrance to DiMillo's floating restaurant.

Bay Mist *(bottom)*

Jennifer Bourque

Casco Bay Island ferries gather at their terminal at the State Pier. A reliable mode of transportation for island dwellers, the ferries are also a tourist favorite in the summer months.

Tall Ship *(opposite)*

Cynthia Lewis

The grace, beauty and romance of a sailing ship fascinates landlubbers as much as true bluewater sailors.

Portland Head in the Fall

Jeanne Couillard

Fall colors provide a framework
as an autumn fog shrouds the
light house at Portland Head.

Lobster Boat *(above)*

William O'Donnell

A load of traps and a tank of gas and this freshly-painted workhorse stabled between the pilings and a wharf is ready to go to sea.

Portland Head Light *(right)*

John Williams
NIKON N 70
KODAK GOLD 100

The architectural symmetry of the lightkeeper's house at Portland Head attests to a style found in variations along the New England coast. Built with a ruggedness needed to withstand the elements, the structures evoke a charm enhanced by their relative desolation. Without the sea at their doorstep, they would seem out of place.

Waterfront Berths

John Williams
NIKON N 70
KODAK GOLD 200

It is easy for boaters and yachts-men to find reasons to like Portland Harbor. For many, a berth at Dimillo's is a summer-long haven.

Summer Sail *(opposite)*

Cynthia Lewis
CANON REBEL
FUJI 200

For those who never go to sea, tall ships are an invitation to free their imagination and con-jure pictures of past glories.

Mighty Tall Ship

Charles Boothby

The Coast Guard's training ship
Eagle is docked at State Pier in
full dress for "Operation Sail
2000."

DiMillo's *(opposite)*

Charles Boothby

When the late Tony DiMillo
moved his popular Commercial
Street restaurant across the street
in the early 1980s, the establish-
ment became the only floating
restaurant north of Boston at
the time.

Portland Observatory

Beverly Phillips
CANON TX
KODAK 400

The Portland Observatory was erected in 1807 as a signal tower to approaching ships. Constructed of heavy timbers in an octagonal design, it recently underwent a major renovation.

Fireworks *(opposite)*

Janet Pullyard

Portland waters are awash with color at a summer celebration.

"The Rose" off Portland Head Light

Michael Leonard

CANON A-1
FUJI ASA 200

"The Rose," one of several tall ships visiting Portland during the summer of 2000, swings majestically past Portland Head Light on the way toward Spring Point and the harbor.

Spring Point Light and Fort Gorges *(top)*

Douglas Leitch
CANON F 1
FUJICOLOR 100

The tall ship, "The Rose," passes between Spring Point Light and Fort Gorges.

Moonrise *(bottom)*

David Bowie
NIKON N 70
FUJI 100

Portland Head Light is the second beacon along the eastern Cape Elizabeth shore. The light, the state's most famous, was commissioned by President George Washington in 1791.

U.S. Coast Guard's "Eagle"

Cynthia Lewis

For the sailors of the "Eagle," theirs is the sense of appreciation, knowledge and the sureness of competency.

Op Sail

Cynthia Lewis

The tall ships were in Portland Harbor and Casco Bay in the Summer of 2000 welcoming thousands aboard and below their decks.

Hanging Out

Timothy Byrne
NIKON F 4
KODAK PORTA 400

Crew members of the Harvey
Gamage gather on the bowsprit
as they tend the foresails
helping bring the tall ship
into harbor.

Op Sail

Charles Boothby

Sails full, a schooner shows off in Portland Harbor.

Piers: New Look in an Old Port *(left and below)*

Charles Boothby

New piers have contibuted to Portland's waterfront revival in the past decade. The Scotia Prince docks here at the ferry terminal while cranes await container ships at dockside.

What's Your Pleasure? *(opposite)*

John Williams
NIKON N 70
KODAK GOLD 200

Motor and sail, impressive yachts tie up along condominiums of Portland Harbor.

FALMOUTH
YARMOUTH
FREEPORT

Anchorage at Portland Yacht Club

Ginger Collins
OLYMPUS
KODAK GOLD 100

Boats lay at anchor between Clapboard Island and the Portland Yacht Club in Falmouth Foreside. Many seasonal sailors from Maine and New England ports gather each August at the Portland Yacht Club for the annual Monhegan Race.

Casco Bay Weekenders

Deborah Dunn

NIKON FM 10
RITE AID 200

Casco Bay, extending from Portland Harbor eastward to Fuller Rock off the southern tip of the Phippsburg peninsula, is a favorite summer playground for boaters. Hundreds of crafts in various lengths and riggings ply the waters around the 200 islands and spiney peninsulas.

Woodlands Country Club

Gail Waitkun

NIKON FM2 70 210MM

A winter ice storm transforms the fairways of Woodlands Country Club into a sea of surreal bubbles.

Yarmouth Harbor *(opposite)*

Scott Conner

NIKON N 90S
FUJICHROME VELVIA 50

Water and boats play as prominent a role in Yarmouth community life as elsewhere along the Maine coat. The combination has long provided artists and photographers with some of their most appealing subject. In Yarmouth Harbor, photographer Scott Conner is at no loss for subject matter.

Royal River *(opposite)*

Shawn Roberts
CANON ELAN II
KODAK GOLD 100

A fall morning begins just off the walkway of the Royal River.

Cottage with a Rainbow

Scott Conner
NIKON N 90S
KODAK ELITECHROME
SELECT 100

Perfect timing favors the photographer in catching a halo over a Yarmouth cottage.

Bridal Bush *(below)*

Scott Conner
NIKON N 90S
KODAK ELITECHROME
SELECT 100

A bridal bush in a Yarmouth dooryard reaches full bloom in time for the wedding season.

Emerald Water of the Royal River *(above)*

Scott Conner
NIKON N 90S
FUJICHROME VELVIA 50

Motorists traversing the bridge over the Royal River get a fleeting glance at the quiet pool below Yarmouth village and the classic profile of the Yarmouth Boatyard.

Cumulus Clouds *(left)*

Scott Conner
NIKON N 90S
FUJICHROME VELVIA 50

Cumulus clouds rise in the breeze, making a sharp contrast with a deep-blue New England sky.

Reflections

Scott Conner

NIKON N 90S
FUJICHROME VELVIA 50

Reflections from the sparkling waters of Yarmouth Harbor dance upon a sailbooat's bow.

Royal River *(following page)*

William Mattern

CANON REBEL
FUJICOLOR SUPER HQ

The Royal River, one of the most prominent geographic features of Yarmouth and Casco Bay, flows out of Sabbathday Lake and Lily Pond in New Gloucester, curling its way toward its outlet at Yarmouth Harbor. Serene and easily navigable by small watercraft along some stretches, there are also rips and small falls which require portages.

Dinghy at Yarmouth Marine
(opposite)

Scott Conner
NIKON N 90S
FUJICHROME VELVIA 50

The combination of water and boats has long provided artists and photographers with some of their most appealing subjects.

Lupines along the Cousisns River

Scott Conner
NIKON N 90S
FUJICHROME VELVIA 50

A field of lupines embellishes the view along the Cousins River.

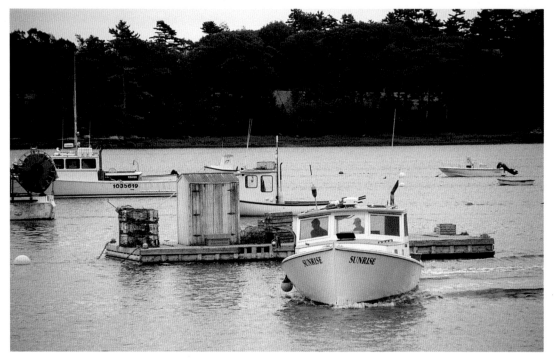

Lobstering *(top and bottom)*

William Mattern

CANON REBEL
AGFACHROME 200

Lobstermen go about the job of unloading the day's catch after arriving back in Harraseeket Harbor.

First Parish Congregational Church *(opposite)*

Scott Conner

NIKON N 50
AGFA ULTRA 50

The First Parish Congregational Church of Yarmouth, with the same unmistakable architectural lines favored by Congregationalists throughout New England, awaits the faithful beneath a golden frontyard pillar.

Bean's Kids Rock Climbing

Elizabeth Hutz
NIKON F2A 50 MM
FUJICHROME VELVIA

After lobsters and pine cones, Maine is perhaps symbolized by the L.L. Bean hunting shoe. The shoe helped give birth to a giant retail and catalog sales complex in Freeport which has earned a worldwide reputation and reach. Today, downtown Freeport is one of the shopping Mecca's of the northeastern United States, and L.L. Bean's is at the forefront of retailing innovation. In the children's sales building at Bean's, what would be more appropriate than a sample of outdoor activities on the inside.

Selling Lemonade

Elizabeth Hutz

NIKON F2A 50 MM
FUJICHROME VELVIA

A lemonade stand is among the sidewalk vendors catering to the hundreds of thousands of shoppers descending on Freeport each summer.

Ready at A Moment's Notice

Michael Leonard
CANON A-1
ASA 100

Fire trucks and rescue vehicles at the Freeport Fire Station stand at the ready.

Marina Harraseeket Harbor

(opposite)

Linda Rector Reeves
MINOLTA FREEDOM ZOOM
KODAK GOLD 200

The wide mouth of the Harraseeket River is sheltered on the seaward side by the Wolfe Neck Peninsula, and is a favorite port for both fishermen and yachtsmen.

"OFTEN
I THINK
OF THE
BEAUTIFUL
TOWN
THAT IS
SEATED BY
THE SEA…"

THE
ISLANDS

Cushing Island from Fort Williams *(left and opposite)*

Claudia Dricot
NIKON N90S
SENSIA II 100

The view from the shoreline below Fort Williams in Cape Elizabeth, looks toward Richmond Island.

Ram Island and Ram Island Light

Claudia Dricot

NIKON N90S
SENSIA II 100

Looking seaward from Cushing Island at the outer edge of Portland Harbor are Ram Island and the old Ram Island Light.

Littlejohn, Moshier, and Little Moshier Islands *(opposite)*

Claudia Dricot

NIKON N90S
FUJI VELVIA

Boats bob off Great Chebeague, one of the more populous of the Casco Bay Islands. The views face northeast toward Littlejohn, Moshier and Little Moshier.

Sunrise at Admiral Perry's House *(opposite)*

Marsha Kessler

CANON ELAN II
FUJI VELVIA 50

Admiral Robert E. Perry, discoverer of the North Pole, spent summers in his home on Eagle Island off the Harpswell peninsula.

The Profile *(left)*

Kelvin Edwards
MINOLTA TX 1
FUJI SENSIA II

Notches in a cliff along a Casco Bay ledge suggests a profile that we've seen before somewhere.

Dock at Eagle Island

Marsha Kessler
CANON ELAN II
FUJI VELVIA 50

The Admiral Robert E. Perry house and island with its nature trails are open to the public, which arrives by way of the dock.

Trap Pulling and Baiting

Marsha Kessler

CANON EOS 3
FUJI VELVIA

Lobstermen work their traps, pulling, emptying and baiting off Little Mark Island, southwest of Bailey Island.

Fort Gorges Across The Harbor *(opposite)*

Claudia Dricot

NIKON N90S
SENSIS II 100

Fort Gorges, built atop Hog Island Ledge, was started in 1858. The harbor landmark is owned and maintained by the City of Portland and can be reached only by private boat.

Sunflowers in Lobster Traps

Marsha Kessler

CANON ELAN II
FUJI VELVIA 50

Marsha Kessler's still life seems so alive that a viewer can feel the sun's warmth and hear the birds.

View from Great Chebeague

(opposite)

Claudia Dricot

NIKON N90S
FUJI VELVIA

Beyond the Moshiers is the entrance to the Harraseeket River and South Freeport on the mainland.

View of Cushing Island

Claudia Dricot

NIKON N90S
SENSIA II 100

The view from the shoreline
below Fort Williams in Cape
Elizabeth—one of seven forts
that once guarded Portland
Harbor.

Jagged Rock *(opposite)*

Claudia Dricot

PENTAX KX
KODACHROME 64

These jagged rocks of Fort
Williams point toward Cushing
Island, and the passage lit by
the Portland Head Light and
the Spring Point Light.

Buoys at Rest . . . Until Spring

Melissa Stufflebeam

Mackeral Cove at Bailey Island is actually shaped like a lobster claw when viewed from above. It is one of the busier lobster ports on Casco Bay.

Lookout Point, Birch Island

Douglas Leitch
CANON F1
FUJI COLOR 100

Birch Island, off Merepoint Neck, is quiet and cold on a sunny winter day. One of summer's island workhorses has been pulled high and dry and awaits spring and a new paint job.

Buoys at Casco Bay Pier

Carolyn Bearce
SEARS SLR
KODAK GOLD 200

A lobsterman's "office" is
unlikely to be short on the
buoys that serve as a fisherman's
signature as well as marking
his traps.

**Shanty, Mackeral Cove,
Bailey Island**

Melissa Stufflebeam

Colorful buoys hang from a
lobster shack on Bailey Island.

CONTRIBUTORS

Paula R. Abbott
84 Northeast Road
Standish, ME 04084
janla@pivot.net
28, 60

Melanie Alden-Roberts
4013 N Woodstock Street
Arlington, VA 22207
glomper@erols.com
54 (2), 57

Carolyn Bearce
18 Tilden Rd
Scituate, MA 02066
126

Charles B. Boothby
P.O. Box167
Limington, ME 04049
51, 62, 76, 77, 85, 86 (2)

Jennifer Bourque
17 Irving Street
Saco, ME 04042
66, 68, 69, 70 (2)

David Bowie
540 Duck Pond Road
Westbrook, ME 04092
dbowie@maine.rr.com
5, 53, 81

Matt Brown
45 Rustic Lane
Portland, ME 04103
rmbinme@aol.com
*8–9, 14, 16 (2), 17, 18, 20,
21, 25, 36, 39, 40, 61*

Timothy P. Byrne
PO Box 1438
Scarborough, ME 04070
22, 84

Mark Conley
1958 Fircrest Drive
Eugene, OR 97403
68

Ginger Collins
458 Memorial Highway
Yarmouth, ME 04097
90

Scott D. Conner
32 Plimouth Way
Yarmouth, ME 04096
scottconneryru12@hotmail.com
*1, 6, 29, 30, 31, 33, 37, 47,
63, 64, 93, 95 (2), 96 (2), 97,
100, 101, 103,*

Jeanne Couillard
29 Lower Methodist Path
Cumberland, ME 04021
72

Claudia M. Dricot
70 Columbus Rd
Cape Elizabeth, ME 04107
iapetuse@javanet.com
*3, 23, 110, 111, 112, 113,
119, 120, 121, 123, back jacket*

Deborah A. Dunn
438 Lewis Road
Harrison, ME 04040
ddunn@megalinl.net
91

Kelvin C. Edwards
12 Mendum Avenue
Kittery, ME 0394 1505
keledw@aol.com
36, 44, 45, 116

Ross P. Geredien
131 Bridge Road
Brunswick, ME 04011
ross@rassgehote.com
48

Diane Hudson
34 Cushman Street
Portland, Me 04102
dhudson777@aol.com
60

Elizabeth M. Hutz
401 Chandler Mill Road
Kennett Square, PA 19348
*11, 15, 46 (2), 104 (2),
105, back jacket*

Marsha Kessler
12 Winter Street
Topsham, ME 04086 1619
kessler@blazenetme.net
114–115, 117, 118, 121

David A. Kirkwood
13 Stoneledge Drive
Portland, ME 04102
lkirkw@aol.com
cover, 27, 34–35, 38, 42

Lila Kirkwood
13 Stoneledge Drive
Portland, ME 04102
lkirkw@aol.com
24

Douglas C. Leitch
P.O. Box 5091
Portland, ME 04101 0791
celtic-aquariane.hotmail.com
56, 58, 81, 125

Michael Leonard
68 Ledgewood Drive
Yarmouth, ME 04096
mleonar1@maine.rr.com
*7, 26, 32 (2), 40, 50, 65,
80, 106*

Cynthia Lewis
51A Kent Street
Newburyport, MA 01950
71, 75, 82, 83

William Mattern
429 Country Way
Scituate, MA 02066
bgmatt@thecia.net
*45, 55, 98–99, 102.
back jacket*

William F. O'Donnell
145 Portland Avenue
Old Orchard Beach, ME 04064
10, 52, 73, back jacket

Beverly Phillips
62 Federal St
Newburyport, MA 01950
drphillips@acuminintl.com
41, 64, 78

Janet Pullyard
272 State Street, Apt 5
Portland, Me 04101
63, 79

Stephen Raymo
66 Pleasant Street
South Portland, ME 04106
20, 49

Linda Rector Reeves
208 Cambridge Drive
Louisville, KY 40214
llrlr@mciworld.com
107

Shawn Roberts
21 Rider Road
Brewer, ME 04412
roberts@m.dmaine.com
94

Rockport Publishers, Inc.
12, 88, 108

Penny Skolfield
38 State Avenue
pskofield@hotmail.com
19

Melissa Stufflebeam
0162 Oak Hill Road
Litchfield, ME 04350
124 (2), 127

Gail Waitkun
8 Falmouth Ridges Way
Falmouth, ME 04105
gderice@maine.rr.com
92

Marcella Wagner
91 Water Street
Stonington, CT 06378 1431
wagnermrcll@ao;.com
59

John D. Williams
140 Elm Street
Marblehead, MA 01945
johnrita@shore.net
22, 43 (2), 61, 67, 73, 74, 87